# THE MAYOR OF MARDI GRAS

A Memoir

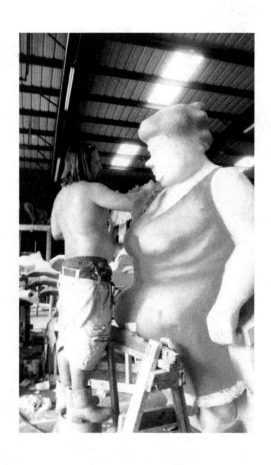

Gregory L. Fischer Jr.

# THE MAYOR OF MARDI GRAS

A Memoir

Make It Write Publishing

Make It Write
Baton Rouge, Louisiana

*This book is a collection of personal memories and stories about my cousin, the late McKinley "Mackie" J. Cantrell, III. It is a true account to the best of my knowledge.*

*Please visit our company website:*
*www.makeitwrite.studio*

*FB: Facebook.com/makeitwrite.studio*

*Some additional photographs of Mackie may be found on Instagram please follow: @themayorofmardigras*

*Published by Make It Write in Baton Rouge, Louisiana*

*ISBN: 978-0-578-38179-4*

**Thanks**
To the Cantrells, for making my life even more colorful.
To the Palmers, for your love.
To my wife, for telling me I should write a book about
**Mackie.**
And to mom because this is my first one.

'

# ACKNOWLEDGMENTS

I haven't left the house much during the last month. It's been too cold to ride my bike or even take Chewy Bacchus Fischer for a walk without bundling up. But now that this book is written, I think it was meant to be. When my wife came home from work four weeks ago and said, "Hey, why don't you write a book about Mackie and call it 'The Mayor of Mardi Gras,'" immediately it felt like divine inspiration. I'd been paused on the other book I was writing for weeks. But I didn't think I could get through writing a book about my cousin so soon after his death. He was one of the most important people in my life.

I tried, anyway. I set my alarm daily for 4:00 a.m. like a man possessed. (It's never been easy for me to wake up in the morning.) Thanks, Carrie for dealing with that kindly. Thanks for your encouragement, support, and understanding. It's been a tough time. Thanks also to Mia and Mackie's Kerri for giving me their photos, approval, and support. And to everyone else: Austin, mom, dad, the Fischers, Costes, Nan and Paran, my wonderful friends who've saved my life, and my stepchildren for letting me spend hours on the weekend working in my office alone when they wanted me to go fly the drone or play Nintendo. Writing would be impossible if I didn't know you were waiting for me right on the other side of that door every day.

I'd also like to take the opportunity to say thanks to the entire Mardi Gras community of artists and float builders. The pandemic has been brutal to this unique, New Orleans industry. I hope things cycle back to normal soon.

I spoke to Mackie's sister Tracy last night, and she shared some memories of her own—of being a kid with Mackie, my older sister Lauren, and my cousin Jennifer—swimming and cutting up at my Aunt Pat's ridiculously large house on Lake Pontchartrain. And I realized that I'm not going to have everyone else's memories of Mackie in this book. But I do hope that it stirs up fond, personal memories in my readers who knew Mackie. My cousin Arthur "Bubba" Coste also shared a hilarious story about Mackie with me on the phone this week—something perfect about softball and getting stoned.

Mackie was such a great, lovable guy that I have no doubt many others could have written their own memoirs about him. I don't want anyone to be disappointed with the contents here. Maybe in the future I can release a new edition with chapters added for others to include their stories. My bond with Mackie was impenetrable in my view, but that's not necessarily exclusive. Lastly, although many tears have been shed during the writing of this memoir, the fact that I got to grieve properly was a blessing. I've spent more hours with Mackie over the past weeks than I have in years.

While writing this I swear I could hear his voice. I've tried to convey those instances by using italics. So, remember that he's right next to you while you read this book, and don't be afraid to have your own conversations with him.

*It's good to be king of your own little town.*
–Tom Petty

# CONTENTS

| | *Acknowledgments* | vii |
| | *Preface* | xiii |
| I | Gravity Culture | 1 |
| II | Harmonious Colloquialisms | 5 |
| III | Dots & Schrempf | 9 |
| IV | Three Mac Cantrells | 13 |
| V | Cousin Camp | 19 |
| VI | Doomsday Defense | 23 |
| VII | AstroWorld | 27 |
| VIII | Illustrations | 31 |
| IX | Brecking Krewe | 41 |
| X | Krewe of Oak | 45 |
| XI | Pastoral Counseling | 49 |
| XII | Van Mourning | 53 |
| XIII | Bayou Couba River Monsters | 61 |
| XIV | Mardi Gras in Siberia | 67 |
| XV | Family Holidaze | 73 |
| XVI | The Funeral | 77 |
| | About the Author | 83 |

# PREFACE

The other night, I was watching this terrific American Master's episode about Helen Keller. I really believe the world misses the extraordinary deeds of Keller. To be deaf and blind and inspire the world would be quite a ride.

It brings me comfort to watch public television or listen to public radio these days because it reminds me of Mackie. Mackie could always interest himself in a radio show or a documentary.

One of the things that struck me about the documentary was her thoughts regarding the death of her teacher, Anne Sullivan, who taught Keller how to communicate. Keller still had much time to live when Sullivan passed, and Keller wrote that she felt as though someone had kicked one leg out from underneath her.

My cousin McKinley "Mackie" J. Cantrell, III's death at forty-seven has hit me harder than anything beforehand. Seven-and-a-half years my senior, he's been my mentor since I was a boy. Mackie was born into the business of Mardi Gras. He was a vital part of New Orleans Carnival culture both "on front street," as he would say, and behind-the-scenes.

I have friends that have lost immediate family members, and I'll admit that I couldn't relate before. Losing someone as close as Mackie cuts to the bone. I'm finally able to see how thin the fabric of life really is. While I'm brokenhearted, the advantage lies perhaps in the realistic attitude I've acquired: *It's gonna end, and it might be today.*

On one hand, I find myself asking what's the point if people suddenly die while striving to achieve a place in the world. Are we all like Sisyphus, having to push the boulder up the mountain over and over again only to watch it roll down just before reaching the top—and having to repeat the upward climb over and over again for eternity? It's dangerous thinking.

On the other hand, maybe I needed to be reminded that I can't take anything with me when I go. Mackie is proving that whether I have everything or nothing, at some point unbeknownst, I'll have no choice but to let it all go.

*Take it light, stab-ah.*

*I know, Mackie.*

In Mackie's death, he's teaching me courage. Thy will be done. And by the way, I'm wrong about Mackie trying to achieve a place in the world. He had not to achieve that. He was a big somebody his entire life.

Yet, the title of this memoir is full of irony. To be clear, this isn't about my relationship with a Mayor of New Orleans who championed Mardi Gras rights (although that would be interesting).

Nor is it about how the real Mayor of Harahan did actually reach out to my uncle to say that Mackie's help after Hurricane Ida in 2021 was invaluable. He stayed and personally handed out generators to as many people as he could. The storm knocked out the electricity for an extended period of time.

Rather, it is about one float builder, who got to rub elbows with Carnival captains and contribute to the grandiosity and fun of Mardi Gras. Of course, there are politics with Mardi Gras like everything else. But "glamorous" is probably the last word I would ever use to describe the year-round work that goes into it.

Even for the Mayor.

# 1     GRAVITY CULTURE

From beads, to brass music, to Carnival Ball gowns, New Orleans Mardi Gras is a sacred ritual. It's comprised of many smaller rituals like placing a King Cake baby or building a ladder for your children.

Once, I left my car parked on the parade route to find out it had been towed. I learned that Mardi Gras is also law. Today, I think of it in terms of the most famous law, gravity. If the city is like the Earth, then Mardi Gras is the sun. And the millions of people across the globe who've made the journey to New Orleans for Mardi Gras are like the stars in an ever-expanding solar system.

But without the gravity of the sun, where would the Earth be? The answer is: probably lost and frozen out in space. That's been the City of New Orleans without Mardi Gras—if not lost, then seriously out of balance.

Similarly, my cousin Mackie was like the sun. And I was the Earth, orbiting around the gravitational force of him. Growing up, that gravity always strengthened or gave way due to life's terms, and as so, it loosened up again five years ago when I left New Orleans and moved to Ascension Parish to become a newspaper editor.

Mackie lent me his big prop trailer for my move. He would've helped me move, I'm certain, but it was February and Carnival Season, 2017, when I took off this time. My dad and brother were there for me.

Things worked out, and I got married in 2020 after finding my Carrie and two new stepchildren, Claire and Charlie. My life pulled further from Mackie's gravity. By that time, he'd been in a relationship with his Kerri for four years, helping her raise Brady and Sophie as well as his own daughter, Mia.

Brady passed away on May 17, 2021. A Brother Martin student, he was seventeen. Young people were in line to the parking lot at St. Philip Neri Church in Metairie to pay their respects. I sat behind Mackie during the service. The pain was incomprehensible.

Then Mackie died on December 27, 2021—a heart attack. I knew he was hurting, but he was always the strongest man I knew. I thought we had decades left together. He never wanted to see a doctor, and heart problems ran on both sides of his family. Someone watched him eat an entire bottle of Tums at once in the weeks preceding his death.

Now I feel like Matt Kowalski, played by George Clooney, in *Gravity*. The tether on my space suit has been cut, and I'm floating towards the unknown. This time for good, I'm afraid.

# II    HARMONIOUS COLLOQUIALISMS

"Constant peril!" Mackie shouted as he stood in a rock and roll guitarist's power stance with a fist clenched high in the air.

I nodded at him like we're all in a state of constant peril. I don't believe that to be the case. But on some level, maybe.

It was 2013, and we were leaving my Bywater apartment on Louisa Street, which had the best balcony. It was a block away from Markey's Bar and the Country Club where clothing was optional at the pool.

Mackie had come over to hang out one night, and I made him watch *Gravity* on my 3D TV. I remember saying that the movie was remarkable because Sandra Bullock's character remains in constant peril throughout the whole thing. Mackie got a kick out of that.

He was known for being excitable and also great at adding harmony to a situation, and it made him a joy to be around. He might yell out something to meet the occasion. For a laugh, he was apt to turning a word or phrase into either a high-pitched David Lee Roth howl or a deep Kirk Windstein growl (depending on the mood). Some famous phrases include:

"Science!"

"Shredfest!"

"Watch Ya Yard!" (also, "Yard-sale"), yard always pronounced 'yawd.'

And "Who Dat!" of course.

But nothing more famously characteristic of Mackie than one in particular: "Stab-ah." Roughly twenty years ago, he started calling everyone Stab-ah. It was endearing, believe it or not. So, let's try something. I'm gonna go ahead and channel the spirit of Mackie right now for a moment (while it's early). And if you're reading this, Mackie wants to say something:

"Stab-ah, I love you. Take a moment."

*          *          *

Each of those special phrases has a story:

"Science!" comes from Mackie's issues with former President Trump. The float den in Kenner could become like an Ancient Greek–gymnasium for political debate from time to time. If you followed Mackie on Facebook, you know all too well his thoughts on politics. And that's not really the story here, either. Although I was always a little awed by how opinionated he was.

I'd like to clear the air and say that I believe simply "love thy neighbor as thyself" was Mackie's true politics.

Next, "Shredfest!" is an easy one. It's a rock concert possibly mixed with a tiny bit of innuendo. "Shut it, shredda"—also related, but this one is attributed to Mackie's sister, Tracy.

Moving on, "Watch Ya Yard," "Yard-sale," (and "Harayard") are all clearly connected by the suffix -yawd. "Watch Ya Yard!" refers to the float den as essentially a construction site, and it's not always super-safe. Sometimes visitors (and workers) need a friendly reminder to take caution. It's versatile though, watch:

> "Mackie, I'm meeting some friends in the French Quarter tonight."
> "Watch ya yard, stab-ah."
> Simple, see? It's a play on "Watch your back."

"Yard-sale!" is what one says on a ski lift when they notice someone's abandoned gear below on the mountain. This also has multiple applications and innuendos.

And "Harayard!" refers to Harahan, Louisiana, where Mackie lived in his grandfather's old home and where my mom, Karen, lived down the street from him.

"Who Dat!" . . . if anyone doesn't know this, they probably aren't football fans.

Lastly, I think I know where "Stab-ah" came from. Mackie's friend Nick said it many, many moons ago. Why? I don't know why. But unlike the others, "Stab-ah" was said in a casual tone most of the time like "dude." Although for me it was usually told in a different way since I love the New Orleans Tennessee Williams Festival. Mackie and I watched *A Streetcar Named Desire* with Marlon Brando one night. So, just like Stanley Kowalski screams, "Stellaaaaaa!" in the movie, I usually got a potent earful of "Stab-ah-hhhhhhh!" whenever Mackie called.

*What's up my brother. Miss you!*
*Miss you too!*

# III    DOTS & SCHREMPF

By 2013, Mackie had worked full time as a Mardi Gras float contractor and artist for over fifteen years. He also owned his own stage lighting and décor business for Carnival Balls. It was called Art Demanded.

I used to love controlling the spotlights with him during the Carnival Ball presentations. What I didn't love was the daytime stage setup and having to pack up all the poles and drapery right after the ball ended. Those were late nights.

We were exhausted, but turning into Dots Diner for breakfast at 3:25 a.m. provided a relief. Mackie never failed at imitating the *yatty* slogan from the Dots commercial: "I'm not your mama, but you're always at home at Dots."

"Mackie, how are you even drinking coffee right now?"

"This won't keep me up." *Know thyself.* Thirty

minutes later he was snoring like a locomotive on the couch. He worked hard.

In high school at Brother Martin, he played football and wrestled. There's a great picture of Mackie standing next to the goalpost in the Superdome in his football uniform during the State Playoffs.

"They called our high school graduating class 'The Class with Class,'" he told me.

Mackie's favorite book in high school was *The Three Musketeers*, by Alexandre Dumas. He liked the character of the younger, "fourth musketeer," D'Artagnan. He told me that he couldn't put the book down and remembered reading it alone in the hallways.

Coincidentally, I'd begun listening to the *Musketeers* on Audible a few weeks prior to Mackie's death—just to tell him I read it. But I didn't let him know in time. For now, I can at least imagine him as a high school kid in a hooded sweatshirt and khakis, sitting in a sunny hallway at Brother Martin, reading.

Even during high school, Mackie was an artist. I remember thinking the drafting board in his bedroom was the coolest thing I'd ever seen (until he showed me a couple Flea licks on the bass guitar). He played bass guitar in a band called Deadpan. He played with other bands, but I kept an old newspaper clipping with a picture of Deadpan. He played bass really well, but he could also play guitar, drums, keys, sing, and write songs.

I used to hang on every note as a kid thirty years ago while he played the ending of "Epic" by Faith No More on his parents' piano in their living room. Ten years ago, I actually tried forming a band with Mackie and his neighbor, Scott.

It never left the jam room. But we did enjoy practicing. I was on bass and vocals, and mostly I remember harmonizing "Can't You See" by the Marshall Tucker Band.

Me: Can't you see?
Mackie: Gonna ride me a southbound, now.
Me: Can't you see?
Mackie: All the way to Georgia, Lord.
Me: What that woman, she been doin' to me!
Mackie: Till the train run out of track!
Me: Oh!

We talked about playing live together. How fun it would have been to rock with him on stage! We used to have our sights on Carrollton Station. Maybe just me. We watched an open mic there once or twice, and the dream was born. Mackie was the first person to ever tell me that I could sing, too. He knew how to instill confidence in others, and at many points in my life I was severely lacking in the confidence department.

Mackie saw the value in others and warned me when he saw me making enemies. I always had a sensitive nature. It helped that he could live in the moment and took his time with me. One day at the float den, I complained to Mackie about a guy in my men's basketball league. "He thinks he's Detlef Schrempf," I said. Or something like that. I was probably mad at the guy for blocking me, honestly. Maybe it was plain jealousy.

To which I recall Mackie's reply: a low, heavy-metal, "Detlef Schrempf!" Quintessential Mackie. "But Greg, wouldn't you rather have him on your team?" he asked.

I paused, hardheadedly. "You're right."

Life is mainly a team sport, and Mackie had so many people on his team. Maybe he was taught that at the float den early on since each Mardi Gras float is like building a small house. And it requires teamwork. Maybe it was in his DNA as a third-generation float builder.

# IV  THREE MAC CANTRELLS

Since the naming tends to throw people off, there are three generations of McKinley J. Cantrell: "Mackie," my cousin; "Mac," his father (who is also my Godfather); and "Big Mac," Mackie's grandfather on his father's side.

Mackie's mother, Kathy Cantrell, is my "Nan" and Godmother. She is my mom, Karen's, twin sister. I call Mackie's father "Paran" because we call our Godparents Nan and Paran in New Orleans.

In 2005, Hurricane Katrina devastated south Louisiana and altered the cultural landscape of New Orleans forever. Mackie and his father were on the front page of the *Metairie Picayune* the following Carnival Season. The headline reads: "Float Builders 'Keep On Keeping On.'"

Three months prior to Katrina, I was taking a journalism class at the University of New Orleans and wrote a brief history of Cantrell float building. Here's an excerpt:

> "Big Mac" Cantrell died on June 7, 2003. His obituary, published online at Nola.com, refers to him as the "World Famous Mardi Gras Float Builder." Nonetheless, Big Mac, according to my Paran, began honing his craft during the Great Depression.
>
> He started working for Carnival float builders known as the Deutschmann Brothers (sometimes spelled without the second "n"), whose family is credited for building the first Rex floats in 1877.
>
> The company name evolved to John H. Deutschmann and Sons, and they were busy working with the Krewes of Hermes, Babylon, and Carrollton while Big Mac was employed there.
>
> After nearly ten years, Big Mac asked for a reference from the owner of the company to purchase a house on David Drive in Metairie. His request was refused. Dismayed, he walked away from them and began working for a float builder and designer known as George Blattny.
>
> Anthony J. "George" Blattny (1897-1971) was a Czechoslovakian immigrant who came to New Orleans in 1918 because of political trouble. Blattny originally worked

for Soulie-Crassons and built for the oldest and major krewes at the time in New Orleans, including The Mistick Krewe of Comus, Knights of Momus, and the Krewe of Proteus.

Big Mac was hired to supervise Blattny's float contracting endeavors. He worked day-in-and-day-out building floats for better pay and treatment. He became masterful at it, and within two years was made a partner.

Those contracts, worth $60,000 in roughly 1955, would be worth $650,000 today. Big Mac was finally able to afford things like property. Eventually, he had enough experience and money to open his own company McKinley J. Cantrell and Sons. Blattny and Big Mac remained friends throughout the rest of Blattny's life.

In 1973, Big Mac began the Krewe of Mardi Gras in Metairie. It paraded for over twenty years, and it showcased his best work. By the way, all those plastic Carnival cups in the kitchen cabinet? The Krewe of Mardi Gras was the first to throw them. Big Mac was also the first to have twinkling lights on the floats.

"You have to utilize the lighting," Mackie

said while I recorded him painting a Voodoo scene on the side of a float one night during Mardi Gras in 2012. "That's what Paw Paw was good about. You're trying to animate with paint to make it look like it's moving at night in the flickering of old flambeaus. Imagine what that must've looked like without all the streetlight that you have today! Totally flickering with the gold leaf poppin'. That's what made Mardi Gras, Mardi Gras. Then it evolved (or devolved)." He laughed.

In 1974, Mackie was born. Mackie's father also started the Krewe of Thor that year, which paraded for nearly forty years. Hurricane Katrina severely affected its membership. Eventually it disbanded. Today, Mac Cantrell Jr. is Captain of the Krewe of Kings, which parades in Metairie. Additionally, he serves on the board for the St. Patrick's Day Parade on Metairie Road, which Mackie also served on.

Nothing lasts forever, except memories. And even in our darkest hour one good memory is said to have the power to save us. What I remember of Mackie's grandfather was that he was sharply dressed with his hair combed to the side while away from the float den.

He smoked a Belair cigarette and drank a tall beer. He called everyone "podnuh," and he worked until practically the day of his passing in his early seventies. His funeral featured the most flowers I've ever seen in one room, mostly coming from the Carnival krewes. He took care of the people who worked for him, and those still alive will testify to that fact. I have witnessed grown men sobbing over his memory.

Kenner's Rivertown district used to feature a Mardi Gras Museum near where the Cantrell's float dens are coincidentally located. I believe the museum closed after Hurricane Katrina due to damage. Among the lavishly sequined costume dresses and feathered headpieces there was a picture hanging on the wall of Mackie's father and his grandfather standing side by side.

During a middle school field trip to Rivertown, I remember feeling so proud to tell my friends that those men were my family. I doubt that all of my classmates even believed me. I imagine my cousin Mackie felt that pride to an even greater degree.

# V    COUSIN CAMP

Mackie was quick to hand out a job, but whether or not someone was there to work, they were welcomed at the float den by him. To say he was a loyal friend would be a grave understatement. And he often had visitors throughout the day. People would drive up and dump their stories on Mackie while he created a prop or painted the side of a float.

The "Mayor of Bucktown" was one of those people. No, there's no real Mayor of Bucktown, but Paul Danna was Mackie's friend who grew up with him in Bucktown, Metairie, and that was his nickname. He visited Mackie practically every week. Bucktown is a small neighborhood on the shore of Lake Pontchartrain, where Mackie grew up. Lakeshore Playground is where he played sports.

Other "mayors" of micro-New Orleans neighborhoods knew Mackie, as well. Donald

"Duck" Lally, for instance, the "Mayor of Hog Alley" worked with Mackie at the den for years and was a close friend. Duck passed away on December 1, 2020 at sixty-five. I know it hurt Mackie because he called me in tears to let me know. The three of us took a bus trip to Houston in 2015 to watch the Saints get pounded by the Texans.

If anyone asked, Mackie was the Mayor of Harahan. Again, not the real Mayor of Harahan, although the City of Harahan has one. But Mackie would put Harahan up against anything New Orleans proper has to offer. Need a mechanic? Harahan. Hardware store? Harahan. Best Veal Parmesan Po-boy? Red Wagon, Harahan. Best Snowballs? Harahan. My younger cousins Carl and Austin get a kick out of that.

All the boy cousins are pretty close on the Coste side of the family. Me and Mackie are kind of like the "middle child" of the generation, which includes Robbie, Bubba, David, Ricky, Mackie, Me, Carl, and Austin. Mackie loved to take weekend getaway trips to Folsom, Louisiana for relaxation on his parent's land.

In 2014 all those guys I just listed spent the weekend there together for "Cousin Camp." The first night we fried fish and played flip-cup with Jack Daniels Honey. It was fun to catch up. It was chilly that night since it was late November. I slept in a tent with Mackie while the rest of them filled up the camper.

In the morning my cousin David was tinkering with the fire, trying to get it started. My cousin Bubba poured some leftover oil on the embers to get it rolling again. Then, suddenly the wind picked up and before we knew it the fire was rushing all over the dry grass. Mackie was scared we might burn down the horse stable, which was void of life at the time (thank God). But you don't want to burn down even an empty horse stable.

"Stab-ah! Grab the end of that hose!" Mackie yelled at me. I had on orange Nikes that turned black. We connected as many hoses as we had to wet the grass around the stable enough to keep the fire away. It was a mess!

We accidentally wound up burning ten acres of land before the volunteer fire department had to step in. Once the fire was out and the land was black as far as the eye could see, we shot skeet and ate more fish. It could've been worse, but we lucked out.

That Christmas we all gave Bubba fire safety gifts. The following year, the grass at the camp grew prettier than ever.

# VI    DOOMSDAY DEFENSE

I could smoke a cigarette and watch Mackie for hours, whether he was making flowers, moving floats, or carving Styrofoam into the Fred Flintstone car or the face of Christ. He had balance like a cat. A low center of gravity and freakish strength could keep him on a ladder for as long as he needed to finish painting or stapling canvas to wood.

I might as well have been sitting in the Sistine Chapel watching Michelangelo paint the Creation of Adam, sitting on an upturned paint bucket on the dirty floor in the middle of all the floats.

It was a holy place to me. The den was at the center of my artistic universe.

My mom always worked around money: casinos, banking, ATMs. My dad worked in insurance. I was pretty certain that art was none of those things. I mean, money is useful. But it's not beautiful. Mardi Gras floats are both beautiful and useful. There's a difference.

I think of Mackie as being an Avant Garde artist because much of what he did required experimentation. Mardi Gras art requires work with many different materials. For instance, working with foam and fiberglass was challenging to learn and didn't always work out. I saw him trash a couple projects in disgust.

But it's a paradox to say that Mardi Gras is Avant Garde because remember, Mardi Gras is still the sun. It's the very center of New Orleans, and the city keeps orbiting. Mardi Gras is archetypal: parade, music, and costumes—over and over again a thousand ways. The messaging is typically based on mythology from Native American to ancient Greek and Roman.

*You know what's Avant Garde, stab-ah? Chewbacchus is Avant Garde.*

*That's true, stab-ah.*

Other than having long hair and a goatee, Mackie wasn't trying to be cool. He just was. He liked mainstream TV Shows that I couldn't stand like *The Voice.* He drove a Nissan truck. He was a Facebook junkie and was extremely comfortable in a golf shirt, cargo shorts, and skateboarding shoes. He really liked Carhartt for winter gear.

I never knew if his sunglasses were expensive

because they were always splattered with paint. They were probably cheap, like ZZ Top suggests. Even though he was Mackie Cantrell, he worked at rejecting self-importance. He cared about others deeply, and he lived modestly day-to-day.

That's not to say he didn't get to experience a number of blessings. This brings to mind a photograph of Mackie as a boy standing with his father and the famous New Orleans musician Dr. John. Mackie always called the late Dr. John by Mac Rebennack. Go figure. Mac. The "good doctor" played the Krewe of Thor after-party in the 1970s for pennies on the dollar today. And Mackie is watching Dr. John play right now above the clouds—or sitting in on guitar—practicing new songs to share with us soon.

\*       \*       \*

If there wasn't much to say, we could listen to talk radio all afternoon and laugh and yell. Mackie could listen to anyone on the radio, but we loved Bobby Hebert and "Spud" McConnell.

We went back in forth imitating Hebert's Cajun accent until we were crying some days. Hebert's storyline had certain parameters. It must be built upon a night out before the Saints game drinking margaritas on Bourbon Street, and the

Saints' "Doomsday Defense" had to be thrown in there.

Mackie: "I gotta tell ya Deke, last night I was at da world-famous Rick's Cabaret in New Arl-ee-ans. And on my third delicious magarida I realize dat da Saints ah supposed ta have da 'Doomsday Defense' . . . But it looks like we da ones dats doomed."

The Hebert bit was born in 2011. By 2011 Mackie was well settled into his own place. He'd inherited Big Mac's old house on Cris Laur Street in Harahan, a quaint one-story house with a lot of bamboo in the backyard for us to cut down. It had a large room in the back of the house for jamming.

Mackie's house was a reward after much toil. There were ups and downs in Mackie's life like any: refusals, risks, figuring out his place, forming a company, disputes, concerts, breakups, vacations . . .

# VII   ASTROWORLD

Although I've lived in southern Louisiana for most of my life, from 1989-93 I lived in Houston, Texas, with my mom. The Cantrells came to visit us. It's some of the fondest memories I have of that time in my life. I remember tagging along with Mackie and his friends in AstroWorld. They were fifteen or sixteen, and I was like eight, but the gravity was strong even then.

I soaked in their interest in girls and their thoughts on being cool. I gained the courage to ride the Texas Cyclone roller coaster. They had a recording studio in AstroWorld where they would produce anyone's performance of a popular song into their very own cassette tape with their name printed on it. I think it was called Big Time Studio. Like the *Musketeers,* Mackie and his friends harmonized "Under the Boardwalk," by the Drifters.

"People falling in love . . . we'll be having some fun . . . under the boardwalk, boardwalk!"

I recorded alone: "Under the Bridge," by the Red Hot Chili Peppers. Mom still calls at odd times during the day and night to play me that recording. My prepubescent voice sings:

"Sometimes I feel like I don't have a partner. Sometimes I feel like my only friend is the city I live in . . ."

Mackie took me to my first metal concert in 1992. Mom and I were visiting the family in New Orleans for Thanksgiving. He was eighteen and I was ten, and we saw Pantera with Crowbar and Trouble at the Municipal Auditorium. It was my first time being patted down and searched on the way in. Mackie laughed when I looked at him like, "What the hell is going on?"

I'll never forget his friend Eric coming to talk to us for a minute in between moshing—shirt off, sweaty. It made me love Mackie for being content to sit behind all the action with ten-year-old me during the show. I looked at my fifth-grade classmates when I returned to school on Monday wanting to say: "Listen up sheep, I have seen some shit."

Once I got over myself, I started taking guitar lessons and got a magazine subscription to Guitar World stat.

I remember the *Fresh Prince, In Living Col-*

*or* culture was extremely popular during that time. Vanilla Ice had me shaving lines in my hair. I had a Mariah Carey cassette. The only other concert I can recall before this intimate, raw metal concert, complete with a pit and stage diving, was MC Hammer with Boyz II Men and Jodeci at the Houston Summit with mom.

The following summer we moved back to New Orleans and lived briefly with the Cantrells while our grandmother was dying of brain cancer. That's when Mackie took me to my second rock and roll experience, the Lollapalooza Festival. It was held on the UNO parade grounds. This time was also amazing but not without a minor hiccup.

I got dehydrated or claustrophobic (or both) right before Rage Against the Machine opened up the festival. I fell to the ground as the crowd pushed forward to begin the show. Mackie quickly scooped me up. He brought me to the side of the stage where a medic put me in an ambulance for a few minutes. Some cool air and water put me right back on my feet.

It was another foundational concert experience. We got to see Alice in Chains, Arrested Development and others. I'm happy to be well-rounded when it comes to music. I eventually became a college radio deejay at KLSU and worked at the station for three-and-a-half years.

I attribute that to Mackie.

Mackie liked all sorts of music, too. And he had a deep understanding of New Orleans music culture. He introduced me to John Boutté. Further, he loved Alex McMurray, Walter "Wolfman" Washington, George Porter, Jon Cleary, Papa Grows Funk, and Joe Krown to name a few. Some days, we talked extensively about the history of New Orleans music and particularly, NOLA metal bands. I don't think most people realize the importance of New Orleans on heavy metal.

*Maybe Zebra is the Avant Garde of New Orleans music, stab-ah?*

*True story.*

# VIII    ILLUSTRATIONS

This chapter features photographs of Mackie over the years
to help illustrate the stories. Much thanks to the Cantrell and
Palmer families for contributing.

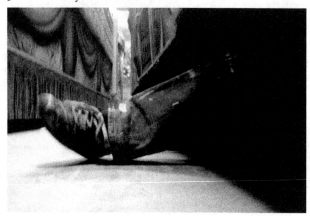

Mackie staples new fringe to the bottom of a Mardi Gras float in 2012. This final touch in the float-making process often becomes a last-minute step.

Mackie and his daughter, Mia, celebrate the Krewe of Kings parade in 2020.

The Mayor of Hog Alley, Donald "Duck" Lally, poses with Mackie while tailgating before the Saints–Texans game in 2015.

Mackie prepares to dock the boat while approaching the camp on Bayou Couba in 2011.

A Flintstones-mobile prop that Mackie made using Styrofoam, wood, canvas, and latex.

Another Styrofoam prop fresh off the carving table. Here Mackie stands several feet behind a classic microphone that he built.

It wasn't unusual to visit the float den and see Mackie covered in Styrofoam like he'd been out in the snow. Here he is using a handsaw to carve out a prop.

A member of the Krewe of Oak, Mackie decorates the balcony at the Maple Leaf Bar for their Mid-Summer Mardi Gras celebration in 2011 for the theme "Love and Meshiness."

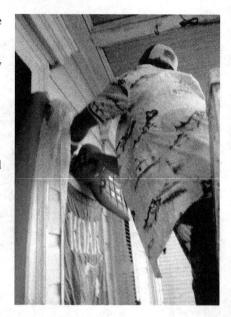

KOAK Mid-Summer Mardi Gras, 2011. I told Mackie once that if you flick off the cameraman, you won't show up on the news. I don't mind if he haunts me for this.

Mackie pets one of the horses at the Cantrell Camp in Folsom, Louisiana while Mia looks on.

The aftermath of a fire that accidentally scorched several acres of land during our Cousin Camp weekend getaway in 2014.

Group photo featuring Brady, Mia, Kerri, Sophie, and Mackie during a Carnival celebration.

Kerri and Mackie pose in front of a sponsored float in the Krewe of Argus parade from the reviewing stands on Causeway and Veterans in Metairie, Louisiana.

Recent Carnival props Mackie created. The "King of Hearts" and Jesus Christ. From the 2022 Krewe of Mad Hatters parade.

"The Night Tripper" Dr. John is pictured here next to a young McKinley Cantrell III and McKinley Cantrell Jr. during a Krewe of Thor after party.

Three Mac Cantrells: Big Mac, Mac, and Mackie. This one was taken during a Krewe of Mardi Gras Carnival ball in 1984.

# IX   BRECKING KREWE

I'd be the first one to say if Mackie had his life all figured out from the jump, but the truth is that Mackie ran from his destiny like every other hero refuses the call. After two years studying studio art at Southeastern Louisiana University (also the alma mater of perhaps the greatest American pianist, Bill Evans), Mackie jumped in the Jeep with his buddy Frey and headed to the mountains in Colorado.

They lived on restaurant work and snowboarding for the next two or three years. But something happened in Colorado that forced Mackie to come home.

The famous English playwright Ben Jonson killed a man in a bar fight during the time of Shakespeare. It's rumored to have been committed out of wrath because the man insulted him. Mackie's ego wasn't half the size of Jonson's. However, one night when Mackie was in

Colorado, someone drew a switchblade on him and his friends at a bar. Mackie, instinctively, threw a billiards ball at his head and critically injured him.

This ordeal must've shaken him to the core though because I never knew Mackie to be a bar fighter. If anything, I'd say he avoided a bar fight like the plague. I know he broke someone's bone once in a wrestling match in high school, but he said it scared the hell out of him. And he said he wasn't proud of it. He could crush me in an arm-wrestling match though. But the Mackie I knew was peaceful—anti-racist, down-to-earth, modest, friendly, and generous.

*I miss you, stab-ah. God, I miss you. I know you're here, man.*

*I'm right here, Fish.*

\*          \*          \*

When Mackie returned home, he continued to run for a while. He worked on the riverfront for some time and as a welder. He learned valuable skills and grit that he would continue to use as an artist and Mardi Gras float contractor for the rest of his life.

If Mackie's career as a Carnival artist was his life's adventure, Big Mac's death was the herald. Most heroes need a mentor to help them get over the fear of starting the adventure. Some just need a big event to join the battle, which could have been the birth of his daughter.

I wish I could tell you that story. Truth is, Mackie had a ton of milestones without me there. That is both comforting and reassuring. My hope is that he led a fulfilling life. If happiness is in the doing, then maybe he was simply spared the confusion and despair that awaits some people in old age.

*       *       *

After Colorado, he traded in his snowboard for a wakeboard. When I was in high school, he took me to the bayous to learn how to wakeboard, and I failed miserably. But Mackie rode a wakeboard like a pro. I preferred to watch him jump high over the wake, back and forth until he got tired. He could ride forever. He also rode the board that didn't have any bindings—wake skating—and made it look easy.

"I didn't realize the beauty of Louisiana until I came home from Colorado," Mackie told me one day. "The mountains can be breathtaking, but the lush greens in Louisiana are something to behold."

I can still see him shaking out his long, wet hair, riding that wakeboard, looking ahead like he was thinking about what trick to pull off next. He looked a lot like Anthony Kiedis. My cousin Bubba used to call him "Chili Pepper" or "Uncle Pepper" because of that. When I was a senior in high school at Rummel, he took me to see Primus at the now defunct State Palace Theatre on Canal Street. My friend who we ran into that night described Mackie as looking "feral."

He was quite a natural athlete and had a winning attitude. But he didn't seem to ever take it too seriously. For instance, at my beckoning he joined a kickball team that I was a part of for a couple of years known as the "Beat-Alls." Once I moved away, I quit playing. But Mackie continued and within the next three years he took them from last place to first.

And by the way, he never got over Colorado. Until his last year, he traveled to Breckenridge every year with his friends from Oak Street. It was a group of probably fifteen people. They planned the trip for right after Mardi Gras each year so Mackie could enjoy it. They called themselves the "Brecking Krewe."

## X   KREWE OF OAK

I enjoyed being at the Maple Leaf Bar in 2011 more than just about anything. It was the best music bar in the city and a short cab ride down River Road from where Mackie and I lived in Harahan. I can't count how many times we watched the Joe Krown Trio with Russell Batiste Jr. on drums and Walter "Wolfman" playing the guitar with his teeth. Walter:

"But these last two dollars, I'm not gonna lose!"

One day that summer, I was working with Mackie at the float den. I remember that we were listening to "Hand In Hand" by Elvis Costello. I went through a brief phase that year where I thought I was Elvis Costello.

I had been fixing this tabletop-sized eagle prop with paper mâché for three days. And we stood there in the afternoon heat, shirts off, my arms elbow-deep in glue. Costello:

"Don't you know I'm an animal?

"But don't you know I can't stand up steady?

"But you can't show me any kind of hell that I don't know already!"

Mackie was going through some mail he'd brought with him from home. He'd just come in from grabbing it out of the "Exploder." He found a letter that looked interesting, and he opened it.

"What you got there?" I asked. He shot me a coy grin.

And he began reading aloud, "You and a guest are hereby cordially invited to the Krewe of Oak's celebration of Mid-Summer Mardi Gras and Carnival Ball . . . the theme this year will be 'Love and Meshiness.'"

My heart began pumping. The Maple Leaf is the starting point of the Mid-Summer Night's Mardi Gras celebration. It marks the middle of the year before the next Mardi Gras. Mackie was well-known at the club. He used to live on Oak Street within walking distance, and his friend John still owns the nearby bike shop NOBS.

"Are you—am I invited—do you want me to go with you?"

The last part of the song, a crescendo, began.

Costello sings: "Hand in hand! Hand in hand! Hand in hand!"

"We going, my brother!" Mackie said. "Hand in hand!" He smiled when I lifted my arms in the air in triumph.

Much of the Krewe of Oak is kept a secret although photos of past royalty hang in the bar. Thousands of people showed up in kinky and elaborate costumes to march across Carrollton Avenue in revelry, but only some got to enter the ball afterwards. Since the theme was "Love and Meshiness," much of the crowd utilized fishnet material into their costumes.

Mackie made a literal fishing motif out of it. He wore an unbuttoned, fish print shirt and white shrimping boots. He wrapped his torso in real fishing net and hung a few, bright lures from it.

That day in August, Mackie and I spent time prior to the krewe's celebration upstairs on the Maple Leaf balcony. We decorated it with red and white drapery to match the "Love" theme. I got to help Mackie hang the KOAK banner and the fiberglass crown he constructed. The bar had become transformed with his carnival-colored drapery.

The night was both a spectacle and a blur. But we marched right up front with the king that year. We also shared a few laughs with

Mackie's friend, Fish. He's the other "Fish," of course. Most people know him as the guy who dresses as the Pope at the Saints games.

We bounced back and forth from the bar to the street where the Baby Boyz Brass Band would not quit. Inside there was a five or six-piece band on stage. Mackie nudged me at one point and said, "Stab-ah, somebody told me that's Stevie Wonder's saxophone player on stage."

*No way.*

# XI   PASTORAL COUNSELING

When I interviewed Mackie for the 2005 article I wrote in college, he was a busy man. He still made time for me. His daughter was a toddler. They lived together in a shotgun house on Oak Street a few doors down from the Maple Leaf Bar. Mackie even lit the backyard with an old, parade-style flambeau for us.

"If you ever want to quit school and come work with me full-time, come on," Mackie said in the flickering torch light. "You'll go back really quick."

He was always there for me with those messages. I recently found a letter he wrote me a few years later when I was close to finishing school:

> Hey Greg,
>     If there ever comes a day where you feel overwhelmed by school loans (God forbid) just have a gander at this story. You left the house

*25-30 minutes ago. I'm listening to talk radio with Pricillus and Maximus. I tune in . . . A woman calls in, and she says (with a baby crying in the background on and off), "My husband and I just got out of school and had a baby. We live and work at a bed and breakfast in exchange for a place to live . . ." The wife works 40 hours a week for $150. The husband drives a school bus for $350 a week.*

*They both have master's degrees in pastoral counseling. WTF is pastoral counseling? They owe $150,000 in loans combined! They're both pastoral counselors in Lexington, Kentucky. What a career choice! Anyway, the woman was asking advice from some (turns out) holy charlatan financial advisor who hangs up on this woman pouring her heart out because he couldn't handle the baby crying in the background! What a dick!*

*It could always be worse. You have made wonderful decisions in your life. Your manner, your education, all beautiful choices. I'm proud to share the same blood with you. Be successful and believe in whatever you do.*
*All the love in the world,*
*Cuz*

*       *       *

*So, Mackie, I believe in telling this account of your life.*

What I can't believe is that I found this letter twelve years after it was written. He could've called and talked to me that night, but he wrote me a letter with a pen on loose-leaf. And I was sentimental enough to keep it.

The irony is that Mackie might as well have been a licensed pastoral counselor for all the visitors he had at the float den every day.

I knew that float building was hard from my summer and winter breaks as a kid. I would work for a week or two at the float den, usually spending my abridged time there making or fixing an old prop using paper mâché. The materials are harsh, not to mention pungent. Old paint gets smelly. Buckets of glue are ice cold during the winter. The temperature is the main problem. You have to find a way to work in the natural climate, which for the most part is either wet and hot or wet and cold in New Orleans.

Lo and behold, I did quit school and work full-time with Mackie at the float den. Lucky for me, it wasn't until after I had completed my graduate coursework. I worked with him full-time for a year in 2011-2012. After that, I moved to Denver and then to Los Angeles not only to pursue my dream of becoming a famous writer, but also to run away from myself.

"I love you brother," he said. "You don't have to go."

"I think I do, Mackie," I replied "I need to take the opportunity and see some new things, at least."

"We got plenty work."

"Thank you, Mackie—"

"—Plenty work…"

"No, I've got to get out of here."

I packed up my Ford Escape and left during the night two days after Mardi Gras.

## XII   VAN MOURNING

"Stab-ah, run to the back of the den over to the left in the little closet with the paint all over it and grab me my cigarettes off the sink, please, and a lighter."

"I got you," I replied. And I scurried through narrow crevices in between massive props and Mardi Gras floats parked tightly together until I reached a dead end: a stack of lumber that was to be used to build a "cute, new unit, podnuh." I had to go back and find an alternate route. Eventually, I always made it to the sink and found the blue pack of Pall Mall 100s and the cheapo transparent red lighter.

I'd refer to the Mardi Gras float construction business as an industry, but it feels funny since you can probably count the number of businesses building floats on two hands. Apologies, what is a float, you ask? I'll put it in words:

A Mardi Gras float is a one or two-story

movable structure made of wood, canvas, latex, metal, electrical wiring, and rubber that carries people and all their "throws" down a parade route.

In order to build a float, first, you have to purchase or construct a steel trailer. They need to be customized via welding in order to place the foundational beams evenly. Mackie could customize since he was a Renaissance Man, by definition.

Basically, larger pieces of lumber make up the beams. (Before the electric saw, the wood was cut with hatchets.) The builder constructs the floor from there, and then the railings. Raised front and back platforms are created, a closet or two for a bathroom, and if it's a two-story float, a staircase, another floor, railings, and so forth.

Another part of this artistic construction is the customary carving of planks to create a bubbly, cloudlike formation out of the sides of the float. We're talking about texture now. I imagine the word "float" has to do with the structures looking like they are floating off the ground. The wheels are well-hidden, and it looks like a big, lit-up cloud from a dream slowly approaching at night.

*Don't forget the props, stab-ah.*
*How could I forget?*

Each float usually features a sculpture on the front, a prop. The most common material for props is probably paper mâché, but Mackie liked to use Styrofoam and spray foam or a combination. Shiny props are made from fiberglass. Props are held up with wooden or metal bases attached to the float. The base is masked with canvas and paint.

But when it arrives in front of you on the street, and the masked riders are throwing beads and trinkets to the crowd gathered below, one notices the float has a motif. This one could be sponsored by a business and features beautiful colors—yellow, blue, and orange. And that one represents the beach and features sand, a beach ball, and a blonde woman in a bikini. Another represents the swamp. It features alligators and crawfish, and an old fisherman.

These motifs are endless, since New Orleans floats first rolled in 1857.

\*       \*       \*

Back at the den. Inhale, exhale, 2011:

"Have you Van Morninged?" Mackie asked me one day over the phone. *Moondance* by Van Morrison was one of the only working CDs we had to listen to at the float den. Good thing it's a wonderful album.

"Is the caravan on it's way? I've already Van Morninged three times. Where are you?" I asked. I'd been painting this radio float, "laying it in," for nearly three hours.

"I had to pick up Mia from school because she wasn't feeling well," Mackie said. "I brought her back to her mom. I'll be there soon!"

"Sorry to hear that, stab-ah," I said. "Okay, see you soon." I don't know if he ever showed up.

Either way, it was a typical day at work. I honestly could've worked there forever if I had my head on straight. I couldn't keep from drinking, personally. I usually began near the end of my workday. Then Mackie and I would meet up on Cris Laur Street at another point in the evening. We'd cap off the tough day in the sun with revelry.

This was easy because I lived a few doors down from Mackie with my mother that year. I left graduate school. I had barely anything except an education, so I slept on my mother's couch and did Mardi Gras art. In the evenings, I remember shooting hoops with Mackie, building fires in the yard, grilling sausages, watching old episodes of *The Midnight Special* on DVD, playing with his dogs Prissy and Max, gallons of daiquiris, and the seat of my SUV wrecked with paint.

I drove a black Ford Escape during that time. It was over ten years old. Mackie had an aged, white Ford Explorer. Neither of our vehicles were in a marquee state. I can see him now in a heavy metal power stance calling his truck the "Exploder."

\*　　　\*　　　\*

*Someone get Mike Rohli a sammich.*

One day we were having a "safety meeting" in the float den. Every time I hear that phrase it brings me joy to think of longtime float contractor Mike Rohli or artist and author of *Carnival Noir* Rene Pierre, who used to always say it and laugh. Pierre and Mackie sometimes split float painting jobs down the middle. They kept up a competitive but loving spirit together. Both Pierre and Rohli have been around the Cantrell den since the days of Big Mac.

Pierre: We need to have a little safety meeting, podnuh.

Mackie: Oh, are you feeling unsafe?

Suddenly, a massive owl flew in the den from

one of the massive entrance doors and passed overhead towards the back. "He's probably hunting for mice," Mackie said.

I shrugged.

"Stab-ah," Mackie said. "Did I ever tell you about the time I found the mice on the float?"

"I don't think you did." I exhaled.

"One morning I was in here by myself, and one or two of the floats that had been on the street needed to be cleaned," he said.

"Right—"

"—They had to roll that day. So, I'm in here, and I'm finishing my McDonald's breakfast. Then, I go to the upper deck of that float. Someone left an ice chest tipped over. I go to grab it, and it's full of a litter of tiny mice. I had to kill them. My instinct set in. People were showing up soon. I couldn't let so and so's wife go up on the float and see a bunch of mice! They would've flipped!"

"Oh, my God," I said.

"So, I smashed them. Probably twenty of them. I felt so bad, stab-ah. It was brutal. I felt brutal."

He was right. It was uncharacteristic of Mackie to hurt animals. I felt bad for him to be placed in that position. At the time, he had a chihuahua named Max, a dachshund named Prissy, and a cat named Sylvio the Slasher at home. Prissy died a few years back of old age. Max died in 2021 of old age just a few months before Mackie.

Sylvio, however, was fated to become an outside cat that bullied the neighborhood. He looked like Sylvester, the cartoon cat. Sylvio attacked Mackie's face violently one day while he was shaving.

## XIII   BAYOU COUBA RIVER MONSTERS

"Stab-ah, you want to go to the camp this weekend?" Mackie asked. "I'm taking Mia out there for her eighth birthday."

I shrugged. "What's it like out there?"

"It's peaceful," he replied. "Takes about a forty-minute boat ride to find it."

"Really?"

"Yep. It's on Bayou Couba, down past Lafitte. What do you say? We'll do a little catfishing. Some cake and ice cream?"

"Yeah, I'm down." And off we went. We may have taken a Friday off of work at the den. Mackie had on cargo shorts, a white polo, and his white shrimping boots. Mia was so little— big smile, small life vest. We went with Mackie's friend Nick, the originator of "stab-ah." Mackie purchased a share in the camp with Nick and a couple other guys at some point.

It was out in the water, basically sitting on a

thin shore of tall cord-grass. It was rebuilt after Hurricane Katrina and protected from the water by a man-made barrier of pilings and oyster shells. They'd built a beautiful composite board pier to dock their boats and fish off of. The camp was two stories. It had electricity from a large, gas-powered generator and running water from a tank that was treated with chemicals and not for drinking.

It was really cozy, actually, and peaceful. But it wasn't fancy, and for someone not used to those elements it was a little dangerous. At the front door hung a real alligator head. A couple of the guys hunted alligators from the camp, seasonally. That involves wrestling and shooting the alligator in the back of the head. Mackie had gone once, he said.

(Strictly in terms of outdoor sporting, if I drew a line and said at the far-right end, we have quintessential country boy and on the left end we have city boy, Mackie was most definitely right-centered.)

The kids at the camp, which other than Mia belonged to Mackie's friends, were used to picking up snakes. I was not. On the first evening, I fished alone on the pier as the sun went down. At some point I put my beer down and realized that an eight-foot alligator had been tracking slowly back and forth in the water in front of me. I got spooked and called it a day.

When I went to pick up my beer an eastern lubber grasshopper hung off the side of the can like a handle. It was black with yellow and red markings and was the length of the can. Eastern lubbers, turns out, were everywhere. It felt like a different planet.

The next day everyone was outside again. "I got something!" one of the guys announced from the pier right before reeling in a long, black eel. He kept it, and Mackie sliced it into sausage-like chunks that were used to bait jugs. They only looked like sausage chunks. This eel was something else. Even with a sharp blade it took much effort to cut it.

A jug is a sawed-off Gatorade bottle or a milk jug. A heavy-duty nylon cord is attached at the cap and fastened with a knot. The other end of the cord features a big fishing hook.

Eventually, we baited nearly twenty jugs. Then, a group of us that included Mackie, Mia, Troy, and his son hopped in a boat and laid a jug-line in the bayou. We went back to the camp where we celebrated Mia's eighth birthday. I have a wonderful video of Mackie lighting the candles and all of us singing to her.

Later, the same group of us from earlier got back in the boat to pick up the jugs. The sky was mostly clear and the moon and stars reflected off the water. Orange and yellow light from the city in the distance made it appear as though it was on fire. The water was still.

People tend to think of a bayou (and I'm guilty of this myself) as a small body of water resembling a swamp. Bayou Couba is more like a wide channel connecting Lake Cataouatche to the north with the larger Lake Salvador to the south.

However, it maintains its swamp-like character by the sheer number of alligators in the area. In the moonlight, it can be difficult to see the jugs, which are labeled with green reflector tape, floating on the water. It's especially difficult if they have a large fish on the hook, taking it up and down or moving it left to right off the line. So, we used a Q-Beam spotlight to see our line.

The most sobering effect of this journey is when I looked down the line at our jugs, wrapped with tape reflecting bright green on top the water. And I realized that we were surrounded by hundreds of bright red reflections, as well.

"Alligator eyes," Mackie said.

"Jesus."

Nonetheless, it was the children who leaned over the boat and pulled up our jugs one by one. On the hooks, we were averaging four-foot catfish. Once in the boat, it was Mackie who wrestled it into an ice chest. A catfish can cut you badly, and it has stingers. But he could handle them without an issue. I held the Q-Beam. Two of our jugs held gars.

"River monsters," Mackie always called them.

One was so strong that it took us all the way to the cord-grass. It used its alligator teeth to ultimately saw off the nylon line and get away.

We fried a lot of fish together, but the last day at the camp we had the best catfish fry I can recall. I can still see Mackie on that day. It was light and warm outside on the bayou, but overcast. Mackie was all smiles in a blue T-shirt and his shrimp boots. He used a nail to hang these giant catfish on a post and an electric knife to fillet them. Nick was on fry duty. Cajuns do know how to spice and lemon-up some catfish. I never made it back to the camp after that day.

# XIV   MARDI GRAS
## IN SIBERIA

I have wonderful memories of Mardi Gras day. Some are vastly different, which is a testament to the different ways one may choose to celebrate the occasion.

For instance, I have fond memories of standing with friends and family at the reviewing stands in Metairie on Causeway and Veterans. This is the place that the Jefferson Parish krewes traditionally "toast" the king and queen. Once, when I was a kid, former Giants First Baseman Will Clark stood next to me at the stands watching the parades with his family. The New Orleans native was one of my heroes. I got his autograph on a paper plate.

A later memory involves being stuck on Saint Charles Avenue bumbling around the Avenue Pub and Igor's after my car got towed. "Stranded and quite okay with it," is a good way to put it. I'd been out all night before and unknowingly parked along the street right on the Zulu route.

Today, I love being at the parades with my wife and stepchildren. The Spanish Town Parade in Baton Rouge ranks among my favorites. I just don't know what Carnival Season is going to be like without Mackie.

COVID-19 has done a real number on cutting short the memories I've been able to make with my family, but it looks like things may be opening back up. Mackie might not be there in person any longer, but the hundreds of floats and props that he's touched will continue to roll for many years. And some of that work will hopefully outlast me.

The city isn't used to being without any visitors. It misses everyone. I think if you ask most Americans, they would say that they feel comfortable in their own city or town. The difference between New Orleans and those other American cities lies in the fact that visitors also feel at home in New Orleans. That's why I think what they say is true about New Orleans being the closest thing to a European city.

I know that it hurt my cousin Mackie not to have his work used in 2021. And he was afraid 2022 would be the same. He was terribly frustrated. The last few conversations we had were either about Saints and LSU football on a downswing, the loss of his stepson earlier in the year, or venting about the politics of closing the city for Mardi Gras.

*The show continues, stab-ah.*

*I don't want to do it without you. Everybody misses you.*

*Go visit.*

*Okay.*

Mackie was rarely ever with me on Mardi Gras Day. He was always wiped out from working. Mardi Gras season is crazy for the float builders. Last minute touches like stapling the fringe to the bottoms of the floats, paint and prop finishes, trash cleanup, port-o-potty issues, and tractor issues come to mind. Gathering tractor drivers for thirty floats is a royal feat in itself, but multiple parades usually roll simultaneously. Another challenge is making sure the floats rolling in the night parades each have a working power generator for lights and music.

\*       \*       \*

It was finally Mardi Gras season, 2012. I'd worked at the den for a full year prior to this day.

"What's going on today?" I asked when I got to work and the den was crowded with people. Men were lined up to pull the floats by tractor on the six-mile journey from the den in Kenner to the beginning of the Metairie parade route.

I'd never seen anything like it.

My uncle Mac asked, "Greggie, you want to jump in the truck and ride with me?"

"Sure!"

Mackie may have been behind us pulling a float on a tractor or he may have been held up at the den, but that ride with my uncle was something special. Imagine leading a procession of thirty floats down busy streets in the middle of the day. We were escorted by a slew of police officers on motorcycles zipping alongside and in front of us, sirens blasting. Each of them nodding hello to my uncle as they passed. Several taking turns coming to the gray Nissan truck's window and inquiring about "ya mom and dem," which is New Orleans for "family."

Just like that, my year of working daily with Mackie was over. Like I mentioned earlier, I left for Denver soon after Mardi Gras even though Mackie made it clear that I didn't have to. I drove to Colorado to live with my sister's family for a few months. I kept in touch, but I missed Mackie a great deal. I even created a blog called "Mardi Gras in Siberia" and wrote vigorously.

After four months I took off further west for Los Angeles. Two months in Los Angeles were gone in a flash, and I honestly didn't know how to live in the big ole world. I couldn't find a job. I was slow to network. So, I called him.

"Hey Mackie, how's it going?"

"It's going great, my brother," he said. "We've got more work than I know what to do with right now. How's it going in LA?"

"It's cool," I replied. "But I'm having trouble finding a job, and I'm running out of money."

"Stab-ah, we could use you around the shop," he said. "Dude, I'm for real. I will fly you in tomorrow if you want to come home and work with me." But I couldn't go. My dream since I was a boy was to have a writing career. Here I was in Los Angeles and hadn't seen nearly enough.

"God, Mackie, I don't think I can do it," I said. "I'm just not done here yet. I have to see it through a little longer. Maybe something will shake loose."

"Alright, stab-ah. Well, I'm here for you, my brother."

That was Mackie, I think, in a nutshell. And it wasn't just how he treated me. It was how he treated people he loved.

*I'm here for you. Come around anytime. You know where to find me.*

## XV  FAMILY HOLIDAZE

Memories from my childhood include Christmas holidays spent with Mackie and my cousins at the Cantrell house on Focis Street in Metairie. Every year on Christmas Eve they had a party that went on late into the night. It involved loud music and a dance floor. I remember it being exciting and often bigger than just our family. Members of the Krewe of Thor were present.

Eventually, I guess everyone got older and people moved on. But my mom's side of the family, including the Cantrells, still congregate each year for Thanksgiving and Christmas. We have a pretty big family—one of those that doesn't like to leave early. Ever hear of a New Orleans goodbye? It's when you go to tell someone goodbye but it turns into a two-hour conversation. We are those people.

We cut up and have fun catching up. The

trends over the last five years include an ugly sweater competition (with trophies). Of course, COVID-19 caused for us to have to miss some of this intense action.

Mackie and I planned to meet this Christmas at his parents' house in Metairie. We talked the day before Christmas Eve. He was driving back to New Orleans after helping his daughter move some heavy things around her LSU apartment. My phone rang:

"Stab-ahhhhhhhh!"

"Stab-ahhhhhhhh!" I replied. "What's up stab-ah?"

"Just driving back from helping Mia move a few things. What's up with you, my brother? How was Disney?"

"Dude, it's exhausting. You're kind of at the mercy of the kids."

"I know," he said. "We really liked SeaWorld. I watched the *Blackfish* documentary, too. But SeaWorld is fun."

"Alright," I replied. "*Blackfish* was awful though."

"It was. Well, listen, am I going to see you on Christmas?" he asked.

"Yeah, I hope so! We're going to get there early because we have to make it back to Baton Rouge to eat dinner with Carrie's family."

"Ten-four my brother. We'll be with Kerry and them in the morning, but we'll swing through early to catch you."

*     *     *

I don't think I'd seen him but once in 2021 although we phoned a few times. He was definitely seething about the cancellation of the St. Patrick's Day Parade and worried about Carnival 2022. We talked about it. He showed immense strength about Brady's passing though. He didn't have to hold it in with me, but he did.

I waited for the call—I guess, expecting him to break down at some point—but it never came. Then, he called in October and asked if I wanted to go to the LSU–Ole Miss game with him, but I had work and declined. What a mistake! We missed each other again on Christmas Day. As I drove my family back home after spending the afternoon at the Cantrells for Christmas, he called just after I passed LaPlace.

"I'm sorry I missed you, stab-ah," he said. "Sucks. I really wanted to see you."

"I wanted to see you too, Mackie. Maybe New Years?"

"Maybe so. I love you. Drive safe my brother."

"Love you too. Merry Christmas."

## XVI   THE FUNERAL

Two days after Christmas my mom called in the morning and broke the news. She was crying. "What do you mean?" was my reply.

I know he's here with me because a couple weeks ago my wife and I were meeting some family for lunch at City Café in Baton Rouge. I was feeling crumby, like "What's the point of life?" Carrie nudged me to listen to the music playing overhead at the restaurant. It was Van Morrison. I knew it was Mackie, there.

Recently when I was choosing an epigraph, I played "It's Good to be King" by Tom Petty on Spotify because I thought it worked well with the title, not to mention Mackie gave me a Tom Petty album for Christmas last year. But what sealed the deal is that after the song played, "Can't You See" played at random right after it. That was our jam.

*This is to honor you, my brother.*

The night of Mackie's wake before the morning of his burial I had a long, vivid dream. Looking back, I think it had something to do with a traditional view of Heaven:

I was in a strange, winding Dr. Suess land. And I heard that I should take a chance on this game over yonder that only cost a quarter but could win a million dollars.

So, I drove there through the mountains. It looked like an ancient temple in ruins. It was a stone foundation, sitting on a grass field. The sky was dark and cloudy.

I had to flick a quarter and try to knock over a large stone wheel that was spinning in place to win the game. It seemed impossible, but to my astonishment I hit the wheel squarely enough to knock it off balance. And it fell.

But that wasn't the end of the game, so I walked up the steps and entered the ruins. It was full of hundreds of tribal people with their faces painted wearing primitive clothing. They kept approaching me aggressively, but I wasn't scared. So, then they reached me they would just sit or stand in place. I walked around each of them slowly like they had become statues.

One man in particular was small. He

had big eyes, and he looked stern. For this part of the game, I was told that I had to gain his approval to win the money. I was among all these strangers and didn't know what to do.

I decided that I would simply try to love everyone and began to pray for each person I laid eyes on, "God, bless this person. God, bless her. Bless him. Thy will be done," etc.—simple prayers.

But family members I recognized like my brother-in-law and my Uncle Mel popped up here and there for some reason, and they warned me like, "I don't think it's gonna happen for you, Greggie. You're wasting your time."

Eventually, it appeared clearly that I was wasting my time. I took their advice and quit the game *(but I made sure my wife and I bought something at the gift shop before leaving—dreams).*

Then, me and Carrie drove away, and on our way home we reached an intersection that looked familiar like Magazine Street in New Orleans by the park. Except, across the intersection was a department store. All of a sudden, a work van drove in front of me and pulled into the store parking lot. Mackie was sharing the front seat of the van with a bald man and a woman. I watched the van stop in front of the store.

"It's Mackie!" I told my wife. "It's Mackie!" I rushed our vehicle across the intersection into the store's parking lot, just as Mackie lifted a box over his shoulder. He appeared to be walking towards the parking lot, maybe to his truck.

He had on sunglasses. It was him, with his long, stringy hair and dark skin. I knew it was him. But that was impossible because I knew that he was dead, and that the night before my wife and I had both experienced seeing him at his wake.

But people kept getting in the way of my car, so I couldn't quite reach him. A family crossed slowly in front of us. Someone with a garden hose splashed water across my windshield, and I yelled, "Get the fuck out of my way!"

I laid my eyes on him one more time as he walked across the parking lot wearing camouflaged cargo shorts, skate shoes, a baggy, red polo . . .

And then I woke up. First, I let my higher power know how cold that was. But then I felt this sense of overwhelming purpose in getting dressed to drive back into New Orleans for the funeral. I thought at least I couldn't lose him that day. I knew exactly where to find him. Nothing could stop me.

Deciphering the first part of the dream (when Uncle Mel popped in to let me know I was wasting my time in those ruins) was harder to do. But I came to realize that I'm going to have to let others guide me from here on out. Mackie did absolutely everything he could for me during his lifetime, and I'm grateful.

*I am whole. I am full. I am complete.*

It really hurt to have to hug him one last time. He looked great though. I read from the Book of Wisdom at the service. I felt full of sincerity. Teardrops spilled on the sheet of paper in front of me as I took it line by line:

*The souls of the just are in the hand of God*
    *and no torment shall touch them.*
*They seemed, in the view of the foolish, to be dead;*
    *and their passing away was though an affliction*
    *and their going forth from us, utter destruction.*
*But they are in peace.*
*For if before men, indeed, they be punished,*
    *Yet is their hope full of immortality;*
*Chastised a little, they shall be greatly blessed,*
    *Because God tried them*
    *And found them worthy of himself.*
*As gold in the furnace, he proved them.*

*And as sacrificial offerings he took them to himself.*
*Those who trust in him shall understand truth,*
*And the faithful shall abide with him in love:*
*Because grace and mercy are with his holy ones,*
*And his care is with his elect. (3:1-9)*


Mackie is buried in a wall at Lake Lawn Cemetery in Metairie. My wife nudged me after the service. She said I should take a flower from the centerpiece on the coffin. I took a decoration instead, a jingly jester's head on a stick. It's on a shelf in my living room. It is Mardi Gras Season, after all.

Those three lines that he said to me when I was in Los Angeles will ring true for the rest of my life, and this goes for all Mackie's friends and family, the City of New Orleans, and anyone who celebrates Carnival:

*I'm here for you. Come around anytime. You know where to find me.*

## ABOUT THE AUTHOR

Author Greg Fischer is the former Editor-In-Chief of the *Weekly Citizen* in Gonzales, Louisiana, *The Chief* in Donaldsonville, Louisiana, and the *Post-South* in Plaquemine, Louisiana, and contributor to *The Times-Picayune* newspaper in New Orleans, Louisiana. He holds bachelor degrees in Creative Writing and Journalism from Louisiana State University. He attended graduate school for Professional Writing at Southeastern Louisiana University, where he served as Editor-In-Chief of the *Gambit* creative writing journal for students. He is currently the owner of Make It Write, a publishing services company in Baton Rouge, Louisiana, where he resides with his wife and stepchildren.

At the float den on Toledano Street with the Mayor of Mardi Gras.